KU-649-328

Henri's father was an excellent horseman who was usually away hunting and hawking. But he loved his son and during his brief visits would dress up, often in a kilt, and perform funny sketches to amuse Henri.

"Father, tell me about the time you won the chase," Henri would plead. He loved to hear his father's tales of hunting and looked forward to riding himself one day.

J759.1 TOU

Famous Children

TOULOUSE-LAUTREC

TONY HART & SUSAN HELLARD

Schools Library and Information Service

S00000017743

VICTOR GOLLANCZ
LONDON

At their family château in Albi, France the Count Alphonse and the Countess Adèle de Toulouse-Lautrec waited excitedly for the birth of their child. A son was born. They named him Henri.

He was a happy baby but his anxious mother soon noticed that he wasn't growing as fast as he should. The doctor was called and he told them the sad news.

"Henri has a rare bone disease which will affect his growth and health."

Henri's mother and two grandmothers made a great fuss of him. They loved to spoil their "little pearl". Although he was often ill, Henri was always good-natured and curious about the world around him.

Count Alphonse, like many aristocrats, was an amateur painter and sculptor.

"That is a wonderful horse, Father. May I have some clay too?" asked Henri.

"Of course," replied the Count. "Try to show the way an animal moves."

Henri enjoyed these shared moments. At four years old he was already able to draw animals using quick strokes and flowing lines.

Henri drew what he saw around him on the family's many estates – horses, dogs, birds and people. "When a woodcock is killed it gives my family three pleasures – shooting, drawing and eating," said his grandmother with a smile.

"I wish I could go hunting, Mother. Will I be able to go soon?" asked Henri.

"I think your hunting will have to be in your dreams, Ri-ri," she replied sadly.

"Never mind," thought Henri bravely, "At least I have able hands to draw my dreams with."

Age 6 - 7

In 1870 when Henri was six years old, his parents took him to Paris. They rented an apartment in an area popular with artists. Henri loved the excitement of the city with its bustling people and interesting places, except for one place – school!

He was sent to the Lycée Fontanes, but his studies didn't go well as he was always thinking of other things. He filled the margins of his school books with wonderful drawings.

He met up with his cousin, Louis Pascal, and they became great friends.

"I have to leave Paris soon," Henri told Louis sadly one day. "We're going to visit some spas to try and cure my illness. I shall miss you, Louis."

Louis answered cheerfully,

"Don't worry Henri, I shall write to you, if you promise to write back and send some of your drawings."

So the cousins kept in touch by letter. Whenever Henri had some news he would write to Louis.

Henri's letters were full of sketches and stories about his travels.

"I have just been to an American Circus. There was a cage full of lions which were very frightening," he wrote.

Age 10

Age 12

Sadly, the cures offered by the spas did not work for Henri and he returned home to Albi. But at least he didn't have to go back to school. Instead his parents employed a private tutor to help him with his work.

Henri still found his studies boring. His tutor would scold him for covering his books with comic pictures of people – caricatures – instead of reading.

"This will not help you pass your exams, Henri."

Henri's Uncle Charles, however, was more sympathetic.

"You have a great talent, Henri. You must use it."

Encouraged by his uncle, Henri's interest grew and grew. Despite frequent headaches and pains in his legs, he worked hard.

"I hope you are pleased with my drawings, Uncle Charles," said Henri. "Any talent I show has been kindled by you."

Age 13

By now Henri was using a walking stick. The problem with his legs became worse when he was fourteen years old. As he was standing up from a low chair his foot became stuck in the crossbar and he fell.

Disaster! His left thighbone broke and his leg needed plaster. He had to move around in a small cart. His recovery was slow but after resting a while at Albi he was able to travel with his mother to different resorts and spent the winter in Nice.

One sunny day, however, Henri was tempted to go for a short walk with his mother. He stumbled and fell into a ditch, this time breaking his right thighbone!

Poor Henri! He needed long months of rest to recover. The doctor then examined him and broke the terrible news.

"Henri's legs have stopped growing."

Henri finally had to accept that he would never ride and hunt like his father. He refused to feel sorry for himself.

"Gracefulness is not my gift," laughed Henri to his many friends, "but drawing is!" Henri had a lively sense of humour and often made fun of himself.

Wherever he went Henri would draw and sketch what he saw. He painted watercolours and started working with oil paints. Painting was no longer a hobby, it had become a way of life.

Henri was critical of his own work and during his recovery in Nice he became very frustrated.

"I am tired of drawing horses and sailors. My landscapes are awful – the trees look like spinach and the sea is the devil to paint."

His father was worried. Henri was usually so cheerful! The Count decided to find expert art tuition for Henri.

"Princeteau is the man you want," said Uncle Charles immediately.

"Of course!" answered the Count. He, too, knew the famous painter and was sure he would help.

Age 15

René Princeteau was happy to teach Henri. He had been born deaf so his speech was strange and clumsy. He could easily understand Henri's feelings of frustration. He and Henri became friends and soon Henri was enjoying drawing his favourite subject again – horses!

Age 16

"First make copies of my paintings to learn new skills," said Princeteau. "Then you can do your own work."

Princeteau was so delighted with the results that he even called one of Henri's drawings "perfect".

Henri wrote to Uncle Charles.

"Princeteau has been raving about

my work. He says that I can imitate like a little ape! I am going to train with Leon Bonnat." Bonnat was a very famous portrait painter.

Age 17

And so at the age of eighteen Henri began to study art formally.

Bonnat was a strict teacher and made Henri work hard.

"Your painting is not bad," said Bonnat of Henri's work, "but your drawing is simply atrocious."

Still, Henri respected his teacher and learned many of

the skills that helped him in the paintings of Paris life, which later made him famous.